# American Slave, American Hero

## York of the Lewis and Clark Expedition

Laurence Pringle

*Illustrations by*
**Cornelius Van Wright
and Ying-Hwa Hu**

CALKINS CREEK
An Imprint of Highlights
*Honesdale, Pennsylvania*

*Dedicated to Dennis, Arlene, Adam,
and Brooke Hirschfelder—steadfast friends
whose lives reflect their ideals, with fond memories
of Vineyard vacations, birthday celebrations, and
countless good conversations since 1972*
—LP

*To Cal, a true modern-day hero*
—CVW and YHH

## Acknowledgments

The author thanks Dr. Sterling Bland, associate dean of the Graduate School and associate professor of English at Rutgers University, Newark, New Jersey, who reviewed the text for accuracy about the lives of slaves in the United States. Thanks also to Jay Rasmussen for fact checking both text and illustrations. Mr. Rasmussen is past president of the Oregon Chapter of the Lewis and Clark Trail Heritage Foundation, and recipient of the National Council of the Lewis and Clark Bicentennial's Outstanding Service Award.

Cover and interior design by C. Porter Designs

CALKINS CREEK
An Imprint of Highlights
815 Church Street
Honesdale, Pennsylvania 18431
calkinscreekbooks.com
Printed in China

Library of Congress Cataloging-in-Publication Data

Pringle, Laurence P.
  American slave, American hero : York of the Lewis and Clark Expedition / Laurence Pringle ; illustrated by Cornelius Van Wright and Ying-Hwa Hu.—1st ed.
    p. cm.
  Includes index.
  ISBN-13: 978-1-59078-282-8 (hardcover : alk. paper)
  1. York, ca. 1775-ca. 1815—Juvenile literature. 2. Slaves—West (U.S.)—Biography—Juvenile literature. 3. West (U.S.)—Biography—Juvenile literature. 4. Lewis and Clark Expedition (1804-1806)—Juvenile literature. 5. West (U.S.)—Discovery and exploration—Juvenile literature. I. Van Wright, Cornelius, ill. II. Hu, Ying-Hwa, ill. III. Title.

F592.7.Y67P75 2005
917.8'042092—dc22

2005037352

First edition
The text of this book is set in 12-point/18-point Caxton.

10 9 8 7 6 5 4

In the 1770s, two boys were born on a Virginia plantation. One became a famous explorer and leader whose name is still celebrated to this day. Today the other is also considered a national hero, but few know his name: York. Little is known about some times in his life, so you will find the word "probably" used occasionally in this, the true story of York.

Long ago, when the United States was a very young nation, a woman who was probably named Rose gave birth to a boy. He was named York, after his father, who became known as Old York. The baby and his parents were slaves. No one knows when York was born because such records were not usually kept for slaves.

York and his parents were owned by the John Clark family of Virginia. The Clarks had six sons, four daughters, and about twenty slaves, and lived on a plantation where they grew crops of tobacco and vegetables.

York was a few years younger than William, the youngest Clark son. As the boys grew up they were probably playmates. Together they explored the Virginia woods and fished its streams. They learned to ride horses and to swim. York must have been a good, trustworthy companion, strong and smart, because at about age twelve he was chosen to be William Clark's personal servant.

4

Instead of working long hours in the fields each day, York tended to the needs of William Clark. He slept in the Clark home. He ate better food and wore better clothes and shoes than the slaves who worked in the fields. However, he was still a slave.

William Clark was his master. Clark later wrote of him as "my black man York."

York could not read those words. Teaching a slave to read or write was forbidden by law in Virginia and many other states.

About the time that York became William Clark's personal servant, John Clark bought a large tract of land in Kentucky, in the fertile Ohio River valley. The Clark family and their slaves settled there in 1785. Everyone, black and white, worked at clearing fields, planting the first crops, and building a house, barn, and fences, as well as cabins for the slaves.

The new Clark home, called Mulberry Hill, was on the western frontier of the young United States. People who settled there were sometimes attacked by Indians. Part of York's job was to protect the Clark family, so he probably learned to use a rifle and became a good shot. (In more settled areas, slaves were not allowed to use firearms.)

7

At age nineteen William left home to serve in the military. He became a lieutenant in the United States Army. During the seven years William was away, York probably served as a house slave at Mulberry Hill. In a 1795 letter, William Clark wrote that York had visited his army camp. Perhaps he brought his master some supplies from home.

Later in 1795 William Clark returned home to help run the family farm at Mulberry Hill, and York once again became his personal slave. In the years that followed, Clark sometimes traveled on family business to New Orleans, New York, and Washington. No doubt York usually traveled with him.

At the turn of the century, in 1800, Clark had his thirtieth birthday. York was in his late twenties. He was tall and powerfully built—and he was in love with a slave from a nearby farm. Their masters gave them permission to marry. A marriage between slaves was a simple ceremony, usually conducted by the master of the house or plantation. No public records were kept of slave marriages, so historians have no information about York's wife's name, when they were married, or whether they ever had any children.

In July 1803, William Clark received a letter from Meriwether Lewis, who had become a friend while they were both serving in the army. It told of President Thomas Jefferson's plan to explore the unmapped West, all the way to the Pacific Ocean. Lewis asked Clark to help him lead this extraordinary expedition. Clark accepted eagerly. He wrote, "My friend I join you with hand & Heart."

While Lewis prepared for the expedition, Clark began to seek the kinds of men they would need for this wilderness adventure. The two leaders agreed that the men should be young, healthy, hard workers, who had experienced living and hunting in the rugged outdoors. Lewis and Clark tried to choose the best men from among the many who volunteered. As a slave, York could not volunteer, or refuse, to go on the expedition. Whether he went was up to his master. William Clark had no doubts. He had relied on York's help for many years. He wanted trusty York at his side.

The Lewis and Clark expedition—called the Corps of Discovery—set out on May 14, 1804, by boat up the Missouri River. York was one of about four dozen men who rowed the Corps's large keelboat and two smaller flat-bottomed pirogues. The boats were heavily loaded with food, clothing, tools, weapons, gunpowder, and lead for bullets. The cargo also included many bundles of beads, scissors, combs, knives, and other items the men could use in trade with Indians.

The Missouri was wide, swift, and dangerous. The boatmen had to avoid branches and sometimes whole uprooted trees swept downstream by the current. At times York and the other men struggled to free a boat that had become stuck on a sandbar. Each day the crew labored many hours, using oars, long poles, or towropes to advance about ten miles upstream.

13

Each morning some of the men set out on foot with their rifles to hunt for the expedition's meat. Meriwether Lewis often explored alone with his Newfoundland dog, Seaman. He collected leaves of plants and made observations about the land and its wildlife. Clark usually stayed aboard ship, estimating distances and taking compass readings that would help him draw accurate maps.

Lewis and Clark, as well as several other members of the Corps, kept journals. They wrote of many things— from pesky mosquitoes to badgers, bison, and other animals they saw for the first time in their lives. They wrote about daily events, dangers, and jobs well done. On June 5, 1804, Clark wrote, "my Servent York Swam to the Sand bar to geather greens for our . . . Dinner . . ." The men ate mostly meat, so having watercress or other wild edible leaves with a meal was a treat—and good for their health.

Later in the summer, Sergeant Charles Floyd became ill, complaining of a terrible pain in his stomach. Clark wrote that of all the men, York was especially helpful. York cared for Floyd as well as he could, but none of the simple medicines brought on the expedition helped. Floyd died on August 20, 1804, and was buried on a bluff overlooking the Missouri.

15

On some days the treeless plains were darkened by herds of bison. The men hunted them for food and also used bison skins to make clothes and warm robes. One day Sergeant Patrick Gass wrote of bison hunting in his journal: "One of our hunters killed one, and Captain Clarke's black servant killed two."

17

In September the expedition paused for three days near the villages of the Teton Sioux while Lewis and Clark met with the leaders of this powerful tribe. One of their goals was to learn about Native Americans and to promote friendly relations with them. However, the Teton Sioux were not friendly. York and the other men kept their rifles ready and barely slept at night. One meeting with the Sioux almost ended in battle. On September 28 the expedition started out again. Eager to get far away from the Sioux, York and the other men pulled hard on their oars.

In early October the expedition camped near a village of Arikara Indians. The Arikara were friendly and pleased with the gifts Lewis and Clark gave them. It was York, however, who most delighted and fascinated the Arikara men, women, and children. Clark wrote in his journal, "Those Indians wer much astonished at my Servent, They never Saw a black man before, all flocked around him & examind. him from top to toe."

As York played with the children, he pretended to be a wild animal that gobbled up people. Clark wrote in his journal that York "made himself more turibal than we wished him to doe." York also showed his great strength. To the Arikara, this powerful black-skinned man was "big medicine," which meant something unexplainable and awe-inspiring.

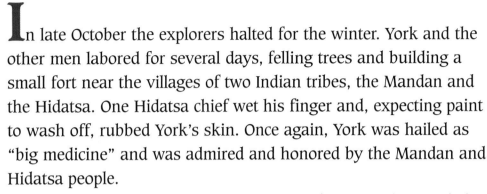

In late October the explorers halted for the winter. York and the other men labored for several days, felling trees and building a small fort near the villages of two Indian tribes, the Mandan and the Hidatsa. One Hidatsa chief wet his finger and, expecting paint to wash off, rubbed York's skin. Once again, York was hailed as "big medicine" and was admired and honored by the Mandan and Hidatsa people.

One December night the temperature fell to 45 degrees below zero Fahrenheit. Even on days when the air "warmed" to zero degrees, the men had to hunt for food. On December 8 Clark, York, and fourteen others killed a deer and eight bison. York and several other men returned with frostbitten feet.

The men often sang and danced after dinner, when Pierre Cruzatte played his fiddle. William Clark had noticed that York was an extraordinary dancer. On New Year's Day, 1805, he told York to dance for an audience of Mandan and Hidatsa. In his journal Clark wrote that the Indians were amused and astonished "that So large a man Should be active."

In early April the Missouri River was free of ice, and the expedition prepared to continue westward. First, however, a dozen men headed downstream in

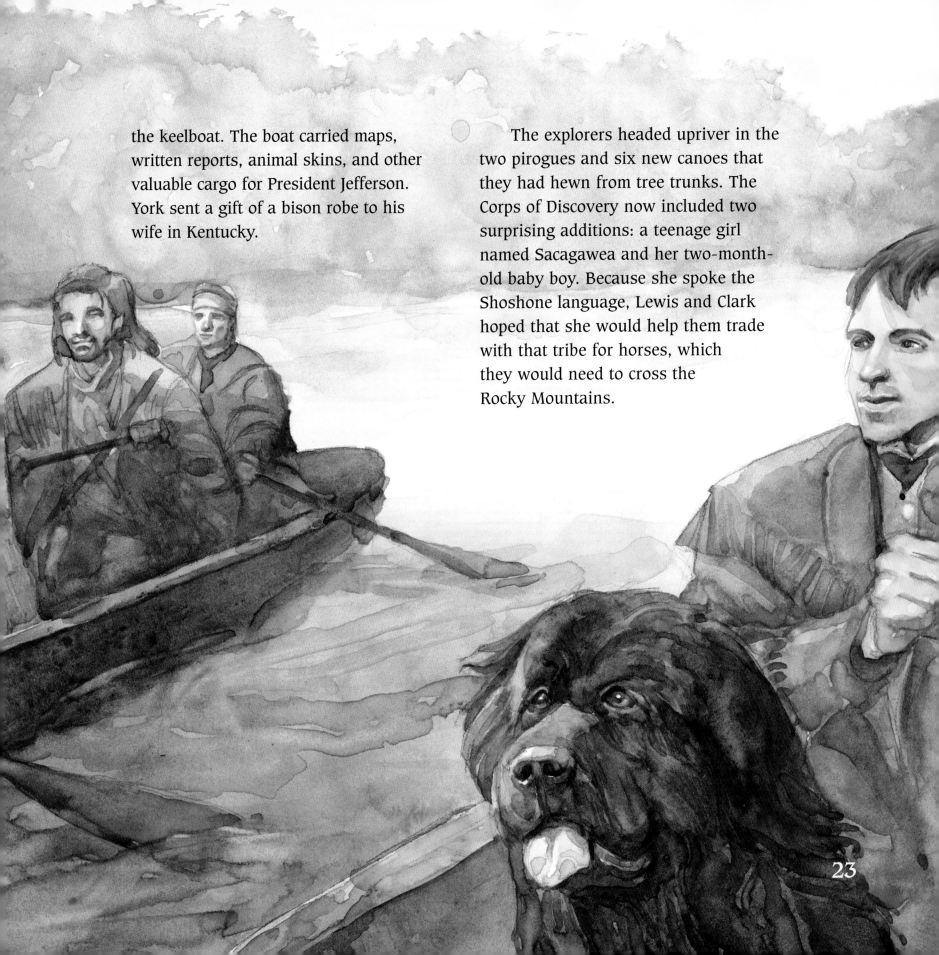

the keelboat. The boat carried maps, written reports, animal skins, and other valuable cargo for President Jefferson. York sent a gift of a bison robe to his wife in Kentucky.

The explorers headed upriver in the two pirogues and six new canoes that they had hewn from tree trunks. The Corps of Discovery now included two surprising additions: a teenage girl named Sacagawea and her two-month-old baby boy. Because she spoke the Shoshone language, Lewis and Clark hoped that she would help them trade with that tribe for horses, which they would need to cross the Rocky Mountains.

The expedition advanced deeper and deeper into wild, unmapped country. The explorers faced dangers from rattlesnakes and grizzly bears. In their daily battle against the Missouri's current, sometimes York and the other men had to jump into the cold water and tow the boats with ropes made of elkskin.

In mid-June 1805, Lewis heard a mighty roar ahead and soon saw a huge waterfall. The explorers discovered that five waterfalls and miles of rapids lay ahead. They labored for many days, hauling the heavy dugout canoes and tons of cargo a distance of eighteen miles around the falls. They limped on feet made sore by cactus spines that pierced their moccasins.

On June 29 a sudden storm caught many of the men out on the treeless plain. Hit by hailstones, some were bruised and bleeding. William Clark, Sacagawea and her baby, and her husband, Toussaint Charbonneau, took shelter under a rock ledge in a ravine. Suddenly a torrent of water rushed toward them.

Clark helped Sacagawea and her baby up the steep side of the ravine, above the rising floodwaters. York soon appeared. He had been hunting when the storm struck, then had gone searching for Clark. He was relieved to find everyone safe. Clark later wrote that York was "greatly agitated, for our wellfar."

In mid-August, towering mountains—
and the threat of winter—loomed ahead.
Lewis hurried forward and finally met
the Shoshone, who had the horses the
expedition needed. The Shoshone,
however, were eager to head east to hunt
bison. Using sign language, Lewis urged
the Shoshone chief, Cameahwait, to wait
for the rest of the explorers. He said that
they included a woman from the
Shoshone's own tribe (Sacagawea),
a man with red hair (Clark), and,
most remarkably, "a man . . . who
was black and had short curling hair."

The Shoshone stayed, and they, too,
found York to be "big medicine." Among
the Shoshone and some other western
tribes, men who had fought well in battle

blackened their faces with charcoal. Since
York was all black, he was considered a
great warrior, more powerful
than his white companions.

Soon the expedition had the horses they needed and a Shoshone man to serve as a guide. The explorers struggled through the snowy, rugged Bitterroot Mountains. Hunters returned empty-handed and food supplies dwindled. The Corps ate meager meals of candles and bear grease.

William Clark and six hunters (probably including York) hurried ahead and met Nez Perce Indians who were digging edible lily roots on a prairie. The Nez Perce befriended the hungry travelers and agreed to care for their horses. They also gave York a special name that meant "black Indian."

27

On October 7 the explorers settled into newly made canoes and set out down the Clearwater River. After struggling against river currents for many hundreds of miles, York and the other paddlers were now happy to be carried downstream toward their goal, the Pacific Ocean. The explorers rushed down the Clearwater to the Snake River and then into the Columbia. Because York could swim, he was probably among those chosen to paddle the canoes through the most dangerous rapids, while men who could not swim walked along the shore.

On November 7, 1805, the Corps of Discovery reached a wide bay just twenty miles from the Pacific Ocean. They had made it! Everyone was in high spirits, even though strong winds and crashing waves trapped them on shore for more than a week. When the weather calmed, they retreated upriver a bit.

On November 24 Lewis and Clark called for a discussion and a vote on where they would build a fort for the winter. Clark tallied the votes in his journal. York's vote was recorded—more than sixty years before slavery ended in the United States and freed male slaves could vote. Sacagawea's vote was also recorded—more than a hundred years before women throughout the United States were given the right to vote. The fact that he was a black slave and she was an Indian woman did not matter to the others. Day after day they had proved their value to the expedition's success.

The majority voted to cross to the southern side of the Columbia and search for a good fort site. They did so, and in December the men built Fort Clatsop, named for the Indians of that area.

They needed York's great strength in constructing the fort, but he injured himself. On December 28, 1805, Clark wrote that York was "verry unwell from a violent Coald and Strain by Carrying meet from the woods and lifting the heavy logs on the works."

During the winter by the Pacific, York often went hunting, especially for elk. From elkskins, York and others made clothes and many pairs of moccasins, which they would need on the journey home. Everyone looked forward to that trek, because rain fell nearly every day. Sleep was interrupted by biting fleas, which infested their blankets and robes. Clark wrote of "haveing my blankets Serched and the flees killed every day." It was probably York, his servant, who went flea hunting!

On March 23, 1806, they left the dreary climate of Fort Clatsop and began to paddle their canoes up the Columbia River. A month later the explorers began to trade elkskins and other items for horses and to travel by land. By late May they had enough horses and were eager to start across the Bitterroots. But the Nez Perce warned them that the mountain trails were still buried under many feet of snow. They would have to wait.

The waiting was difficult, partly because the explorers had trouble getting enough food. The hunters did their best, and Lewis and Clark continued to trade with the Nez Perce for food. But they had little left to offer the Indians.

They did, however, have York, a man greatly respected by the Nez Perce. Twice York was sent on trading missions. Twice he returned with a surprising amount of food. Before the second trip, Lewis and Clark cut the brass buttons from their military uniforms. With these and a few other small items, York and a man named Hugh McNeal traded for three bushels of edible roots and some bread made of lily roots. Lewis praised the men and expressed pleasure at "the return of a good cargo."

After crossing the mountains, the expedition split into two groups, aiming to explore different river valleys. Clark's group, including York, canoed down the Yellowstone River until it joined the Missouri. Clark continued to draw maps and to name features of the landscape after members of the expedition. He named a river that flowed into the Yellowstone for York. (In 1805 he had named a cluster of islands in the Missouri "York's Eight Islands.")

On August 12, 1806, the two groups led by Clark and Lewis reunited on the Missouri, and the explorers sped downstream. York continued to help feed everyone. The journals report that he shot an elk and a bison for food.

The explorers had disappeared into the unknown for twenty-eight months. When they met trading boats heading upriver, they learned that nearly everyone had given them up for dead! Cheering crowds greeted the explorers when they reached the river town of St. Louis on September 23, 1806. The expedition's return was celebrated at dinner parties, first in St. Louis and later in Washington and other cities. Everyone praised Lewis and Clark's leadership, but all members of the Corps of Discovery—including York—were hailed as national heroes.

Eventually the men of the expedition were rewarded with double pay and many acres of land. Because he was a slave, York received nothing. He also had no choice but to settle in St. Louis with William Clark in 1808, when his master began working there for the government.

York asked Clark for permission to work back home, near his wife. Clark refused but allowed York to visit her for a few weeks. York stayed several months, however, and returned to St. Louis reluctantly. York's attitude upset Clark, who wrote to his brother, "I gave him a Severe trouncing the other Day."

Clark gave up on York as a personal servant and sent him to work driving a freight wagon for the Clark family in Kentucky. The owner of York's wife moved to Mississippi with his slaves, so York probably never saw her again. At some point, perhaps as long as ten years after the expedition's return, Clark finally gave York his freedom. He also gave him a wagon and six horses as a start in the freight-hauling business. However, York's business did not succeed. White farmers and businessmen of those times did not often hire freed slaves.

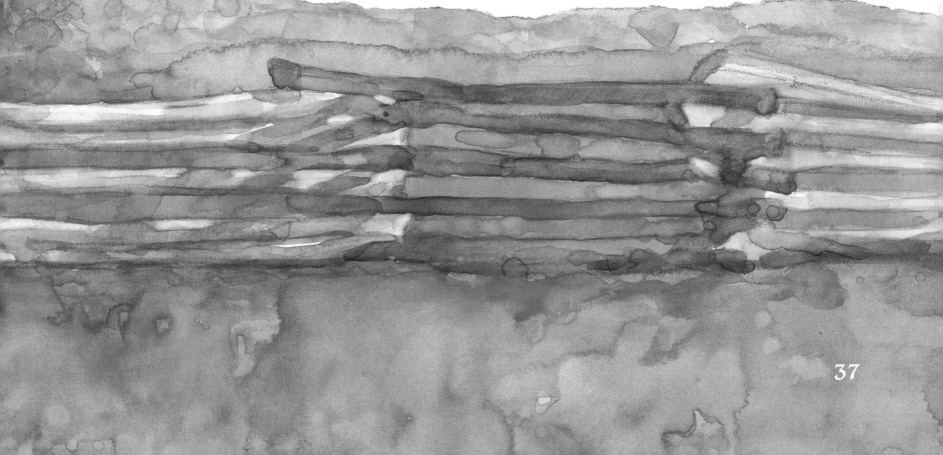

Sometime before 1832, York died of the disease cholera. Some historians believe that York was on his way to St. Louis, in hopes of rejoining William Clark, when he died.

Details of York's death and his burial place are mysteries, as are those of countless other slaves. But the journals of the Lewis and Clark expedition reveal some important truths about York. Like the other explorers, York endured extreme heat and cold, suffered injuries and illness, risked his life many times, and contributed to the success of an expedition that is still considered the greatest in United States history. He was both a slave and an American hero.

---

In 2001, long after his death, York was promoted to the rank of honorary sergeant, Regular Army, by President William Jefferson Clinton.

## Author's Note

With the 2002 publication of *Dog of Discovery: A Newfoundland's Adventures with Lewis and Clark*, it seemed that I would never again write about the most remarkable expedition in United States history. Then I noticed that there were more than a dozen books about Sacagawea, at least six about Seaman the dog, but few about York. And one title for young readers contained several errors.

York was hero enough without distorting history. My research for *American Slave, American Hero* relied on two main sources: *In Search of York: The Slave Who Went to the Pacific with Lewis and Clark* by Robert B. Betts and *The Journals of the Lewis and Clark Expedition*. Edited by Gary E.

Moulton, this authoritative edition of the journals was published in thirteen volumes between 1983 and 2001 by the University of Nebraska Press (most of the quotations in the book are from this source). Robert Betts's book was published in 1985, but a revised edition, published in 2000, is most valuable. It includes new information, written by historian James J. Holmberg, about the lives of York and Clark after the expedition.

Holmberg also wrote an introduction to an excellent children's book published in 2004: *York's Adventures with Lewis and Clark: An African-American's Part in the Great Expedition* by Rhoda Blumberg.

## Index